Donald Trump Biography Book: His Excellency, The Most Iconic Figure in American political history, The man Redefined Politics, His Life Story and current Issues including His Assassination Attempt.

All rights reserved. No part of this publication may be, transmitted, or distributed in any means or form, including photocopying, recording, or other electronic or mechanical methods possible, without the prior permission of the publisher, except in the case of brief quotations embodied in critical reviews and certain other non-commercial uses permitted by copyright law.
Copyright © Peter Clarke, 2024.

Table of Contents

Table of Contents
Introduction
Chapter 1
    Early Life and Business Beginnings.
    Background: Childhood and Family.
    Early Business Ventures
    Initial Successes and Growth of the Trump Organization.
Chapter 2:
    Political Rise and 2016 Presidential Campaign.
    Political Beginnings: Early Political Involvement and Public Persona.
    Early Political Involvement
    Building a Public Persona
    2016 Campaign: Key Moments, Strategies, and the Unexpected Victory.
    Key Moments
    Strategies
    The Unexpected Victory
Chapter 3
    Presidency and Key Policies
    Domestic Policies: Tax Reforms, Deregulation, Healthcare, and Handling of COVID-19.
    Tax Reforms.
    Deregulation
    Healthcare
    Handling of COVID-19

Foreign Policies: Major Decisions on Trade Agreements, Climate Change, and International Relations

Trade Agreements

Climate Change

International Relations

Chapter 4

Controversies and Impeachments

Allegations and Public Image: Accusations of Sexual Misconduct and Public Controversies.

Accusations of Sexual Misconduct.

Public Controversies

Impeachments:

First Impeachment

Second Impeachment

Chapter 5

Post-Presidency Challenges and 2024 Campaign

Legal Battles: Lawsuits, Criminal Charges, and Ongoing Legal Issues

Lawsuits and Civil Litigation

Criminal Charges and Indictments

Financial Implications

2024 Campaign: Key Developments, Campaign Strategies, and Significant Events

Campaign Announcement and Strategies

Key Developments and Events

Campaign Dynamics and Media Coverage

Chapter 6

Legacy and Public Impact

Cultural Impact: Influence on Popular Culture and Media Portrayal
Media Representation
Influence on Popular Culture
Iconic Symbols and Imagery
Impact on U.S. Politics
Changes in Republican Party Dynamics
Societal Divisions and Polarization.
Conclusion

Introduction

In the tapestry of American history, few figures have sparked as much intrigue, controversy, and debate as Donald J. Trump. His rise from a real estate developer to the 45th President of the United States is a story that captures the essence of modern American life—where celebrity, media, and politics intersect in ways that challenge conventional boundaries. Trump's journey is emblematic of a new era where personal brand and political ambition intertwine, creating a complex legacy that continues to captivate and polarize the nation.

Born on June 14, 1946, in Queens, New York, Donald Trump grew up in an environment where ambition and assertiveness were the currency of success. From a young age, he was groomed to take over his family's real estate business, the Trump Organization, which was founded by his father, Fred Trump. The early chapters of his life were marked by a blend of privilege and pressure, shaping a personality that would become both larger-than-life and deeply divisive.

Trump's entry into the world of real estate was not merely a continuation of his father's work; it was a bold reinvention. With a combination of aggressive marketing, high-profile deals, and an innate sense of self-promotion, he transformed the Trump Organization from a modest local enterprise into a global brand synonymous with opulence and audacity. His ventures, including iconic properties like Trump Tower and Trump International Hotel, were not just real estate projects but statements of his ambition and flair for the dramatic. This early success laid the groundwork for a public persona that would eventually become a central feature of his political career.

As the 2016 presidential election approached, Donald Trump's name was already a fixture in the American cultural landscape. Known for his role on "The Apprentice," a reality television show where he played the role of a tough, no-nonsense businessman, Trump had cultivated an image of success and decisiveness. His foray into politics, initially perceived by many as a publicity stunt, quickly evolved into a serious and unprecedented campaign. The 2016 election was a political earthquake, characterized by its unexpected twists and the emergence of a candidate who defied traditional political norms.

Trump's campaign was a masterclass in modern political strategy. Leveraging his celebrity status, he captured the attention of a nation weary of traditional politics. His rhetoric, often brash and unapologetic, resonated with a significant portion of the electorate who felt alienated by the political establishment. His ability to dominate media coverage, both through traditional outlets and social media, allowed him to bypass conventional campaign strategies and connect directly with voters. The 2016 victory was not just a personal triumph for Trump but a watershed moment in American politics. His presidency marked a dramatic shift in policy and tone, challenging established norms and altering the political landscape.

His domestic policies, including significant tax reforms and deregulation efforts, were designed to stimulate economic growth but also sparked considerable debate over their long-term implications. His approach to healthcare and the handling of the COVID-19 pandemic were central to his administration's achievements and controversies.

On the international stage, Trump's presidency was characterized by a reevaluation of traditional alliances and agreements. His decisions to withdraw from the Paris Agreement on climate change and the Trans-Pacific Partnership, as well as his unconventional diplomacy with North Korea, were pivotal moments that redefined U.S. foreign policy.

However, Trump's presidency was also marked by significant controversies. His administration faced two impeachments, a historical first for any U.S. president, reflecting deep-seated divisions within the country and the contentious nature of his leadership.

The allegations of sexual misconduct and the tumultuous aftermath of the January 6th Capitol attack further complicated his legacy, underscoring the polarized reactions to his time in office.

As Trump transitioned from the presidency, his post-presidential years were no less eventful. Legal battles, including multiple lawsuits and criminal charges, added to the ongoing narrative of his public life. His 2024 presidential campaign, driven by a blend of fervent support and substantial opposition, highlighted his continued influence and the enduring debates about his role in American politics.

This biography aims to provide a comprehensive exploration of Donald Trump's life, from his early years and business ventures to his political career and beyond. It seeks to unravel the complexities of a man whose impact on American society and politics is profound and multifaceted. Through a detailed examination of his successes, controversies, and legacy, this book offers insights into how one individual's journey can shape and reflect the broader currents of a nation's history.

Chapter 1

Early Life and Business Beginnings.

Background: Childhood and Family.

Donald John Trump was born on June 14, 1946, in Queens, New York City, to Mary MacLeod Trump and Fred C. Trump. His father, Fred, was a successful real estate developer, while his mother, Mary, was an immigrant from Scotland. The family lived in the Jamaica Estates neighborhood, an upper-middle-class area in Queens. Donald was the fourth child among five children of his parents.

From a young age, Trump was exposed to the world of business through his father's real estate ventures. Fred Trump's business primarily focused on developing and managing residential properties in Brooklyn and Queens. Donald grew up observing his father's work, which likely influenced his interest in real estate.

Trump attended schooling in Forest Hills, Queens at Kew-Forest School. His early years were marked by a competitive nature and a desire to stand out. At age 13, he was sent to the New York Military Academy, a private military school in Cornwall-on-Hudson, New York. His parents believed that the structured environment would help him channel his energy more productively.

During his time at the academy, Trump's leadership qualities began to emerge. He was known for his assertiveness and leadership in various school activities and sports.

After graduating from the New York Military Academy in 1964, Trump enrolled at Fordham University in the Bronx. His time at Fordham was relatively short as he transferred to the Wharton School of the University of Pennsylvania two years later. At Wharton, Trump pursued a degree in economics, focusing on real estate. The Wharton School is known for its rigorous business program, and Trump's education there provided him with a strong foundation in finance and real estate.

Early Business Ventures

Donald Trump's business career began in earnest after he graduated from Wharton in 1968. He joined his father's real estate business, which was then called the Trump Organization. Initially, Trump was assigned to work on projects in Brooklyn and Queens. These were mostly residential properties, including apartment complexes and single-family homes.

One of Trump's first major projects was the renovation of the Commodore Hotel in Midtown Manhattan. The hotel was in a state of disrepair, and its location in the heart of New York City presented a significant opportunity.

Trump negotiated a deal with the city to renovate the property and rebranded it as the Grand Hyatt Hotel. The project was a major success, leading to a substantial increase in the hotel's profitability and boosting Trump's reputation as a savvy businessman.

Following the success of the Grand Hyatt, Trump expanded his business interests beyond the confines of residential properties. He began to acquire and develop commercial real estate, including office buildings and hotels. One of his notable early successes was the development of Trump Tower, a 68-story skyscraper located on Fifth Avenue in Manhattan.

Completed in 1983, Trump Tower became an iconic symbol of Trump's growing influence in the real estate industry.

The building housed luxury apartments, office spaces, and retail stores, and it further solidified Trump's status as a prominent real estate developer.

Trump's real estate ventures were not limited to New York City. He expanded his portfolio to include properties across the United States and around the world. Trump's business strategy involved acquiring distressed properties, renovating them, and then rebranding them to attract high-profile tenants and buyers. This approach allowed him to leverage his brand name effectively, turning underperforming assets into profitable ventures.

In addition to real estate, Trump diversified his investments into other sectors, including casinos and resorts. One of his major forays into the casino industry was the development of the Trump Plaza Hotel and Casino in Atlantic City, New Jersey. The casino opened in 1984 and was followed by several other casino ventures in Atlantic City. Trump's involvement in the casino industry helped to further establish his reputation as a high-profile businessman.

Initial Successes and Growth of the Trump Organization.

The Trump Organization, under Donald Trump's leadership, experienced significant growth during the 1980s and 1990s.

Trump's business acumen and aggressive marketing strategies helped to expand the organization's reach and influence in the real estate market.

Trump's success in real estate was also accompanied by a growing media presence. He became known for his larger-than-life personality and his flair for self-promotion.

Trump's public persona was bolstered by his frequent appearances in the media and his involvement in high-profile projects.

His business achievements and his charismatic personality made him a popular figure in both the business world and the entertainment industry. The Trump Organization's growth was characterized by a series of high-profile real estate deals and developments.

Trump continued to acquire and develop prime properties, including luxury hotels, office buildings, and residential complexes. His ability to secure financing for large-scale projects and his knack for negotiating favorable deals contributed to the organization's success. Trump's real estate ventures were not without challenges. The industry faced periods of economic downturns and fluctuations, and Trump's business empire was impacted by these market conditions.

However, Trump's resilience and strategic decision-making allowed him to navigate these challenges and continue to expand his business interests.

In addition to his real estate ventures, Trump ventured into various other industries, including entertainment and branding. He became known for his role as the host of the reality television show "The Apprentice," which premiered in 2004. The show further enhanced Trump's public profile and contributed to his brand's visibility.

Throughout his career, Trump's approach to business was marked by a willingness to take risks and a focus on leveraging his brand name. His ability to successfully navigate the complexities of the real estate market and his knack for marketing and self-promotion played a crucial role in the growth of the Trump Organization.

By the early 2000s, the Trump Organization had established itself as a prominent player in the real estate industry, with a diverse portfolio of properties and a strong brand presence. Trump's success in business laid the foundation for his subsequent ventures into politics and media, shaping his trajectory as a public figure.

Donald Trump's early life and business beginnings were characterized by a combination of family influence, educational background, and entrepreneurial drive. His early ventures in real estate and his ability to navigate challenges contributed to the growth of the Trump Organization and established him as a prominent figure in the business world.

Chapter 2:

Political Rise and 2016 Presidential Campaign.

Political Beginnings: Early Political Involvement and Public Persona.

Donald Trump's journey into the world of politics began well before his 2016 presidential run. His early involvement in political matters and his public persona played a crucial role in shaping his eventual bid for the presidency.

Early Political Involvement

Donald Trump's first notable foray into politics began in the 1980s when he considered running for office, although he did not take any serious steps until the 1990s. In 1987, Trump publicly explored the possibility of running for president as a Republican, but he did not follow through with a formal campaign. His political ambitions seemed sporadic over the years, as he frequently expressed opinions on various issues through interviews and public appearances.

Trump's political affiliations have been fluid over the years. Initially, he was registered as a Republican, but he changed his party affiliation several times.

In 1999, Trump switched to the Reform Party, which was founded by Ross Perot, a businessman and former presidential candidate. Trump's involvement in the Reform Party was short-lived, as he left the party in 2001 and rejoined the Republican Party.

In the 2000s, Trump continued to make public statements on political issues, often expressing conservative viewpoints. He voiced opinions on topics such as immigration, trade, and foreign policy, which resonated with many conservative voters. During this period, Trump also began to establish himself as a media personality through his role as the host of "The Apprentice," a reality television show that further raised his public profile.

Building a Public Persona

Trump's public persona was a crucial element in his rise to political prominence. His persona was characterized by a combination of self-promotion, controversial statements, and a larger-than-life image. Trump's style of communication, often direct and unapologetic, helped him stand out in the media landscape.

One of the key aspects of Trump's public persona was his frequent use of media appearances to express his opinions. He was known for making bold and sometimes inflammatory statements, which generated significant media coverage.
Trump's willingness to speak his mind and challenge established norms contributed to

his growing visibility and appeal to a segment of the population that felt disillusioned with the political establishment.

Trump's success as a television personality also played a role in shaping his public image. "The Apprentice," which debuted in 2004, featured Trump as a no-nonsense businessman who evaluated contestants based on their performance. The show's tagline, "You're fired," became synonymous with Trump's tough approach to business and leadership. This image of decisiveness and authority resonated with many viewers and helped to solidify Trump's brand as a successful and influential figure.

By the early 2010s, Trump had established himself as a prominent media personality and public figure. His statements on various political issues, combined with his high-profile media presence, laid the groundwork for his eventual entry into the 2016 presidential race.

2016 Campaign: Key Moments, Strategies, and the Unexpected Victory.

The 2016 presidential campaign marked a significant turning point in Donald Trump's political career. His campaign was characterized by a series of key moments, strategic decisions, and an unexpected victory that defied many predictions.

Key Moments

The 2016 campaign began with Trump announcing his candidacy for president on June 16, 2015. His campaign launch speech was notable for its controversial remarks about immigration, particularly his comments about Mexican immigrants.

Trump described some Mexican immigrants as "rapists" and criminals, which drew widespread criticism but also resonated with a segment of voters who felt that their concerns about immigration were not being addressed by other politicians.

Another significant moment in Trump's campaign was his performance in the Republican primary debates.

Trump's debate style was unorthodox and often combative. He frequently interrupted his opponents and used blunt language to make his points. His approach to the debates, combined with his willingness to challenge established Republican figures, helped him stand out in a crowded field of candidates.

Trump's campaign also faced significant controversy over his statements and actions. One of the most notable controversies occurred in October 2016 when a 2005 recording surfaced in which Trump made lewd comments about women. The recording, known as the "Access Hollywood" tape, featured Trump bragging about groping women without their consent.

The tape led to widespread condemnation and calls for Trump to withdraw from the race. Despite the backlash, Trump remained defiant and continued his campaign.

Strategies

Trump's campaign employed several key strategies that contributed to his success. One of the most important strategies was his use of social media, particularly Twitter. Trump's frequent tweets allowed him to communicate directly with his supporters and bypass traditional media channels. His tweets were often provocative and designed to generate media coverage and public discussion. This approach helped Trump maintain a high profile and keep his message in the spotlight.

Another critical strategy was Trump's focus on key battleground states. The campaign targeted states with significant electoral votes that were considered crucial for winning the presidency. Trump's team concentrated on states like Pennsylvania, Michigan, and Wisconsin, where he appealed to working-class voters who felt left behind by the economic changes of the previous decades. Trump's message of economic nationalism and his promises to bring back manufacturing jobs resonated with many voters in these states.

Trump's campaign also leveraged his outsider status as a key selling point. Throughout the campaign, Trump positioned himself as an outsider who was not beholden to the political establishment.

This image appealed to voters who were frustrated with what they saw as a dysfunctional and corrupt political system. Trump's rhetoric emphasized his willingness to challenge the status quo and take on entrenched interests.

The Unexpected Victory

Despite numerous predictions of a Clinton victory, Trump's campaign achieved an unexpected and historic win on November 8, 2016. The election results defied many polls and analyses that had predicted a Clinton win. Trump's victory was marked by his success in key swing states and his ability to mobilize a significant portion of the electorate.

Trump's win was attributed to several factors, including his appeal to working-class voters, his effective use of social media, and his ability to tap into widespread dissatisfaction with the political establishment. The election also highlighted the deep divisions within the American electorate, with Trump's populist message resonating with a substantial portion of the population.

In the aftermath of the election, Trump's victory was met with both celebration and controversy. Supporters praised his achievement as a triumph of outsider politics and a rejection of the political establishment.

Critics expressed concerns about the implications of Trump's presidency for American democracy and values.

In summary, Donald Trump's political rise and his 2016 presidential campaign were marked by a series of significant events, strategic decisions, and an unexpected victory. His early political involvement, combined with his distinctive public persona, laid the foundation for his campaign. The campaign itself was characterized by key moments, unconventional strategies, and a surprising outcome that reshaped American politics.

Chapter 3

Presidency and Key Policies

Donald Trump's presidency, from January 20, 2017, to January 20, 2021, was marked by a series of significant domestic and foreign policy decisions. This chapter examines the key policies implemented during his time in office, providing an in-depth look at how his administration approached various issues both within the United States and on the global stage.

Domestic Policies: Tax Reforms, Deregulation, Healthcare, and Handling of COVID-19.

Tax Reforms.

One of the cornerstone achievements of Donald Trump's presidency was the passage of the Tax Cuts and Jobs Act of 2017. This legislation, signed into law on December 22, 2017, was the most significant overhaul of the U.S. tax code in decades. The reform aimed to stimulate economic growth through various changes to the tax structure. The tax reform included substantial reductions in corporate tax rates.

The corporate tax rate was lowered from 35% to 21%, to encourage businesses to invest more in the U.S. economy and to make American companies more competitive internationally. Supporters argued that the lower corporate tax rate would lead to increased job creation and higher wages for workers.

For individuals, the reform temporarily reduced income tax rates across several income brackets. The standard deduction was nearly doubled, providing a tax cut for many middle-class families. However, the reform also included limits on certain deductions, such as those for state and local taxes (SALT), which affected taxpayers in high-tax states.

Critics of the tax reform argued that it disproportionately benefited the wealthy and corporations, contributing to increased income inequality. Additionally, the tax cuts were projected to add significantly to the national deficit, raising concerns about long-term fiscal sustainability.

Deregulation

Trump's administration pursued an aggressive deregulatory agenda aimed at reducing the number of federal regulations and easing restrictions on businesses. This approach was based on the belief that excessive regulation stifles economic growth and innovation.

One of the key actions taken was the rollback of regulations implemented under previous administrations, particularly those related to environmental protections and financial oversight. For example, the Trump administration repealed the Clean Power Plan, which aimed to reduce carbon emissions from power plants. Instead, it promoted policies favoring the use of fossil fuels.

In the financial sector, Trump signed legislation rolling back parts of the Dodd-Frank Act, a comprehensive regulatory response to the 2008 financial crisis. The rollback aimed to ease regulations on smaller banks and financial institutions, with the argument that these institutions were overly burdened by regulatory requirements.

Supporters of deregulation claimed that these actions would lead to increased economic growth and job creation by allowing businesses to operate more freely. However, opponents argued that the reduction in regulations could lead to negative consequences for public health and the environment.

Healthcare

Healthcare policy was a major area of focus during Trump's presidency. One of his key goals was to repeal and replace the Affordable Care Act (ACA), also known as Obamacare. While a full repeal did not occur, Trump and congressional Republicans made several significant changes to the healthcare system.

In 2017, Trump signed an executive order aimed at expanding access to short-term health insurance plans, which are less regulated than ACA-compliant plans. This move was intended to provide more affordable options for people who did not qualify for ACA subsidies or who found ACA plans too expensive.

Additionally, the Trump administration worked to eliminate the individual mandate, a key provision of the ACA that required individuals to have health insurance or face a penalty. The mandate was effectively eliminated with the passage of the Tax Cuts and Jobs Act of 2017, which set the penalty to $0 starting in 2019.

Despite these changes, efforts to fully repeal the ACA faced challenges in Congress, and many provisions of the law remained in place. The Trump administration's approach to healthcare was characterized by a focus on reducing federal involvement and increasing market competition.

Handling of COVID-19

The COVID-19 pandemic emerged as a major challenge during Trump's presidency. The administration's handling of the pandemic was a subject of intense scrutiny and debate.

Early in the pandemic, Trump faced criticism for his response to the outbreak, including the initial downplaying of the virus's severity and mixed messages about the virus's spread.

Trump frequently emphasized the importance of reopening the economy and expressed optimism about the virus being under control.

In March 2020, the Trump administration declared a national emergency, which allowed for the allocation of federal resources to combat the pandemic. The administration also implemented travel restrictions, including a ban on travel from certain countries.

The White House Coronavirus Task Force, led by Vice President Mike Pence and comprised of health experts, played a central role in managing the federal response. Daily briefings were held to provide updates on the virus and discuss mitigation strategies.

One of the controversial moments in the pandemic response occurred when Trump suggested using disinfectants or ultraviolet light as potential treatments for COVID-19. This comment was widely criticized by medical professionals and led to concerns about public health safety.

By the spring of 2020, the administration shifted its focus to developing and distributing vaccines. Operation Warp Speed, a public-private partnership, aimed to accelerate the development, production, and distribution of COVID-19 vaccines. The program successfully led to the emergency use authorization of several vaccines, including those developed by Pfizer-BioNTech and Moderna.

Overall, Trump's handling of the pandemic was characterized by a mix of economic priorities and public health measures, with significant debates about the effectiveness and consistency of the administration's response.

Foreign Policies: Major Decisions on Trade Agreements, Climate Change, and International Relations

Trade Agreements

Trade policy was a major focus of Trump's presidency, and his administration made several significant changes to U.S. trade relations. One of the most notable actions was the renegotiation of the North American

Free Trade Agreement (NAFTA), which had been in place since 1994.

In 2018, Trump initiated negotiations with Canada and Mexico to update NAFTA. The result was the United States-Mexico-Canada Agreement (USMCA), signed into law in January 2020. The USMCA aimed to address issues such as intellectual property rights, labor standards, and environmental protections.

The agreement included provisions to benefit U.S. farmers, workers, and manufacturers, and was seen as a key achievement of Trump's trade policy. Another major trade decision was the imposition of tariffs on steel and aluminum imports from various countries, including China.

Trump justified these tariffs as necessary for national security and to protect American industries. The tariffs led to retaliatory measures from other countries and created tensions in global trade relations.

Trump's administration also engaged in a trade war with China, marked by the imposition of tariffs on billions of dollars worth of Chinese goods. The trade war aimed to address concerns about intellectual property theft, trade imbalances, and unfair trade practices. The conflict led to a series of negotiations and agreements, culminating in a Phase One trade deal signed in January 2020.

Climate Change

Climate change policy was another significant area of focus during Trump's presidency. Trump's administration took several steps to roll back environmental regulations and withdraw from international climate agreements.

One of the most prominent actions was Trump's decision to withdraw the United States from the Paris Agreement, an international accord aimed at combating climate change. The Paris Agreement, adopted in 2015, sought to limit global warming to well below 2 degrees Celsius above pre-industrial levels. Trump announced the U.S. withdrawal in June 2017, citing concerns about the economic impact of the agreement on American businesses and workers.

In addition to withdrawing from the Paris Agreement, the Trump administration rolled back various environmental regulations, including the Clean Power Plan, which aimed to reduce carbon emissions from power plants. The administration also relaxed vehicle fuel efficiency standards and sought to expand drilling and mining on federal lands.

Supporters of these actions argued that they were necessary to protect U.S. economic interests and promote energy independence. Critics, however, expressed concerns about the potential long-term impacts on the environment and global climate efforts.

International Relations

Trump's approach to international relations was characterized by a focus on "America First" policies, which prioritized U.S. interests and questioned longstanding alliances and agreements.

One of the key features of Trump's foreign policy was his emphasis on reducing U.S. military involvement abroad. Trump frequently criticized the cost of U.S. military engagements and called for greater burden-sharing by allied nations. His administration sought to negotiate new agreements with allies to share defense responsibilities and reduce the U.S. military footprint in various regions.

Trump's administration also pursued a more confrontational stance toward Iran. In May 2018, Trump withdrew the United States unilaterally from (JCPOA), the Joint Comprehensive Plan of Action, an international agreement aimed at limiting Iran's nuclear program. The withdrawal led to increased tensions between the U.S. and Iran, with both countries engaging in a series of confrontations and sanctions.

Another significant aspect of Trump's foreign policy was his approach to relations with North Korea. Trump made headlines with his meetings with North Korean leader Kim Jong Un, seeking to address the issue of North Korea's nuclear weapons program.

Despite three high-profile summits, the negotiations did not lead to significant progress on denuclearization.

Overall, Trump's presidency was marked by a series of bold policy decisions, both domestically and internationally. His administration's focus on tax reform, deregulation, and healthcare reflected his priorities for economic growth and reducing federal involvement.

On the international stage, Trump's policies were characterized by a mix of assertive trade actions, climate change rollbacks, and an unconventional approach to diplomacy. The impact of these policies continues to be a subject of debate and analysis.

Chapter 4

Controversies and Impeachments

Donald Trump's presidency was marked by numerous controversies and significant political events, including two impeachments. This chapter explores the allegations of sexual misconduct that plagued Trump's public image, as well as the detailed accounts of the two impeachment processes he faced while in office.

Allegations and Public Image: Accusations of Sexual Misconduct and Public Controversies.

Accusations of Sexual Misconduct.

Throughout his public life, Donald Trump faced numerous allegations of sexual misconduct. These accusations span several decades and involve a range of allegations from unwanted touching to rape. The first major wave of these allegations became widely known during the 2016 presidential campaign.

In October 2016, just days before the second presidential debate, a recording from 2005 surfaced in which Trump was heard making lewd and boastful comments about women. In the "Access Hollywood" tape, Trump bragged about kissing women without their consent and using his celebrity status to touch them inappropriately. He infamously stated, "You can do anything... Grab 'em by the pussy." This tape provoked widespread condemnation from politicians, public figures, and the general public.

Following the release of the tape, several women came forward with allegations against Trump. These women claimed that Trump had sexually assaulted or harassed them, with allegations ranging from groping to more severe accusations of rape. In response, Trump denied all allegations, labeling them as false and politically motivated.

His responses included aggressive denials and accusations that the claims were part of a coordinated attack on his character.

One notable case involved writer E. Jean Carroll, who claimed in the middle of the 1990s that Trump had raped her. Carroll's claim gained significant media attention, and she sued Trump for defamation when he denied the allegation and dismissed her account publicly.

Carroll's legal battles with Trump continued over the years, leading to high-profile court cases and significant media coverage. The allegations of sexual misconduct significantly impacted Trump's public image, fueling debates about his suitability for public office and his treatment of women.

Despite the controversies, Trump maintained a loyal base of supporters who often dismissed or downplayed the accusations as part of broader attacks on his presidency.

Public Controversies

In addition to the sexual misconduct allegations, Trump's presidency was marked by a series of public controversies. His approach to communication, particularly through social media, played a central role in many of these controversies.

Trump's frequent use of Twitter to communicate directly with the public led to numerous inflammatory and controversial statements.

His tweets often addressed political opponents, media outlets, and international leaders, sometimes leading to diplomatic incidents or heightened tensions. For example, Trump's derogatory remarks about various countries and leaders, including North Korea's Kim Jong Un and several Latin American nations, drew criticism and concern from both domestic and international observers.

Another major controversy during Trump's presidency was his response to the racial justice protests that erupted in the wake of George Floyd's death in May 2020. Trump's rhetoric and actions regarding the protests were often seen as divisive. His decision to use federal law enforcement officers to clear peaceful protesters from Lafayette Square in

Washington, D.C., to facilitate a photo op at a church drew widespread condemnation and accusations of authoritarianism.

Additionally, Trump's handling of the COVID-19 pandemic sparked significant controversy. Critics argued that his administration's response was marked by inconsistent messaging, a focus on reopening the economy over public health, and a general downplaying of the severity of the virus.

Trump's public comments and actions regarding the pandemic, including promoting unproven treatments and his eventual dismissal of the pandemic task force, were points of contention throughout his presidency.

Overall, Trump's presidency was characterized by a series of controversies that influenced public opinion and contributed to the polarized political climate of the time. His unorthodox style of communication and contentious policies often placed him at the center of heated debates.

Impeachments:

Detailed Accounts of the First and Second Impeachments, Including Key Events and Outcomes

First Impeachment

The first impeachment of Donald Trump began in late 2019 and was primarily driven by accusations that he had abused his power as president. The key event leading to this impeachment was a whistleblower complaint regarding Trump's interactions with Ukraine.

In July 2019, Trump held a phone call with Ukrainian President Volodymyr Zelensky. During the call, Trump urged Zelensky to investigate his political rival, Joe Biden, and Biden's son, Hunter Biden, who had been involved with a Ukrainian gas company. Trump also suggested that the investigation could be tied to the release of military aid that had been delayed by his administration. This phone call was subsequently reported by a whistleblower, who raised concerns about the propriety of Trump's actions.

The House of Representatives launched an inquiry into these allegations, focusing on whether Trump had used his office to pressure a foreign government for personal political gain. The inquiry led to public hearings and testimonies from various officials, including former U.S. Ambassador to Ukraine Marie Yovanovitch and former National Security Council official Fiona Hill. Their testimonies provided evidence of a campaign to coerce Ukraine into launching investigations that would benefit Trump politically.

On December 18, 2019, the House of Representatives voted to impeach Trump on two articles: abuse of power and obstruction of Congress. The abuse of power charge was based on Trump's solicitation of Ukraine to interfere in the 2020 presidential election. The obstruction of Congress charge stemmed from Trump's refusal to cooperate with the impeachment inquiry, including his refusal to provide documents and allow witness testimonies.

The impeachment was largely divided along party lines. All Democrats supported the articles of impeachment, while the majority of Republicans opposed them. Trump was impeached by the House, making him the third president in U.S. history to be impeached. The case then moved to the Senate for trial.

The Senate trial began in January 2020, with Chief Justice John Roberts presiding over the proceedings.

The trial featured arguments from House impeachment managers, who presented evidence and called for Trump's conviction and removal from office. Trump's defense team argued that the impeachment was politically motivated and lacked merit.

On February 5, 2020, the Senate acquitted Trump on both charges. The vote fell short of the two-thirds majority required for conviction. The majority of Senate Republicans argued that Trump's actions did not constitute impeachable offenses and that the House had not provided sufficient evidence to warrant removal from office.

Second Impeachment

The second impeachment of Donald Trump occurred in early 2021, following the events of January 6, when a mob of Trump supporters stormed the U.S. Capitol to nullify the 2020 presidential election results. The storming of the Capitol resulted in significant damage, numerous injuries, and the deaths of several individuals.

The attack was widely condemned as an assault on democratic institutions and the peaceful transfer of power. In the aftermath of the Capitol riot, the House of Representatives introduced a single article of impeachment against Trump, charging him with incitement to insurrection.

The article alleged that Trump had encouraged the violent attack through his false claims of election fraud and inflammatory rhetoric.

Specifically, Trump's speech on January 6, in which he urged his supporters to "fight like hell" and "march to the Capitol," was cited as evidence of his role in inciting the violence.

On January 13, 2021, the House voted to impeach Trump for a second time. This impeachment marked the first instance in U.S. history where a president was impeached twice. The vote was again largely along party lines, with ten Republican representatives joining Democrats in supporting the impeachment.

The Senate trial for the second impeachment began on February 9, 2021, following Trump's departure from office.

The trial focused on whether Trump's actions and statements leading up to and during the Capitol riot constituted an incitement of insurrection. The prosecution presented evidence of Trump's role in fueling the attack and the direct connection between his rhetoric and the violence that occurred.

Trump's defense team argued that the impeachment was an unconstitutional attempt to punish a former president and that his speech was protected under the First Amendment.

They contended that Trump's words did not directly incite the violence and that he had no intent to incite insurrection.

On February 13, 2021, the Senate acquitted Trump on the incitement of insurrection charge. Although seven Republican senators joined Democrats in voting to convict, the vote still fell short of the two-thirds majority required for conviction. The acquittal allowed Trump to remain eligible for future public office, including the possibility of running for president again.

Chapter 5

Post-Presidency Challenges and 2024 Campaign

After Donald Trump left the White House in January 2021, he faced a turbulent period marked by significant legal troubles and an ambitious campaign to return to the presidency in 2024. This chapter delves into the various challenges he encountered, the complexities of his legal battles, and the dynamics of his 2024 presidential campaign, including a dramatic assassination attempt and strategic developments.

Legal Battles: Lawsuits, Criminal Charges, and Ongoing Legal Issues

Lawsuits and Civil Litigation

Donald Trump's post-presidency period was dominated by numerous legal battles. These lawsuits spanned a range of issues, including allegations of financial misconduct, defamation, and sexual abuse.

One of the most prominent legal cases was brought by E. Jean Carroll, who accused Trump of sexually assaulting her in a dressing room at a high-end department store in the 1990s. Carroll initially sued Trump for defamation after he denied the allegations and labeled her as a liar. In 2023, a New York jury found Trump liable for both defamation and sexual abuse, ordering him to pay Carroll $83.3 million in damages. Trump disputed the ruling and posted a $91.6 million bond, opting to appeal the verdict. This case was notable not only for the substantial damages but also for the high-profile nature of the accusations against Trump.

In addition to Carroll's lawsuit, Trump faced several other legal challenges. The New York Attorney General's office conducted a comprehensive investigation into Trump's financial practices. The inquiry focused on whether Trump had engaged in fraudulent activities by inflating the value of his assets to secure loans and deflate them to lower insurance premiums.

This investigation led to a civil lawsuit seeking penalties and damages against Trump and his organization.

Trump also dealt with multiple lawsuits related to his business practices and public statements. For instance, he faced defamation suits from various individuals and organizations who claimed that his statements had harmed their reputations. The legal landscape was further complicated by ongoing investigations into his business dealings and the financial operations of the Trump Organization.

Criminal Charges and Indictments

Trump's post-presidency legal issues were not limited to civil cases. He faced several criminal indictments that had significant implications for his political career and personal life. Trump was found guilty of 34 felony counts of falsifying company records in May 2024.

These charges related to hush money payments made to adult film actress Stormy Daniels to influence the outcome of the 2016 presidential election. The conviction was a historic moment, as Trump became the first former president of the United States to be found guilty of a crime.

The legal troubles did not end there. Trump was also indicted in various jurisdictions on multiple felony counts related to his handling of classified documents and efforts to overturn the 2020 election results. The cases involved allegations of mishandling sensitive information and attempts to subvert the democratic process. These indictments further complicated Trump's legal situation and attracted widespread media attention.

In addition to the criminal charges, Trump faced civil suits related to accusations of sexual misconduct and financial fraud. In 2023 and 2024, he was found liable for defamation and sexual abuse in separate civil cases.

These rulings added to the mounting legal pressures and financial burdens he faced.

Financial Implications

The legal battles had substantial financial implications for Trump. By March 2024, his campaign had expended over $100 million on legal fees. The cost of defending against multiple lawsuits and criminal charges placed a significant strain on his financial resources. Additionally, potential damages and penalties from ongoing legal cases further impacted his financial stability. The financial burden also extended to Trump's business ventures.

Legal setbacks and increased scrutiny of his financial practices affected his ability to engage in new business opportunities and impacted existing operations.

Despite the challenges, Trump continued to assert his innocence and maintain his position as a prominent political figure.

2024 Campaign: Key Developments, Campaign Strategies, and Significant Events

Campaign Announcement and Strategies

On November 15, 2022, Donald Trump announced his candidacy for the 2024 presidential election. The announcement marked the beginning of a high-stakes campaign with several strategic elements aimed at securing his return to the White House.

Trump's campaign strategy focused on consolidating his base of loyal supporters and addressing key issues that resonated with conservative voters. Central to his campaign was the theme of populism, emphasizing his commitment to challenging the political establishment and advocating for policies aligned with conservative values. Trump's rhetoric often included strong anti-immigration statements, criticism of the political elite, and appeals to nationalism.

Social media played a crucial role in Trump's campaign. He continued to use platforms like Truth Social, which he founded after being banned from Twitter and other social media sites.
Trump's direct communication with his supporters through social media allowed

him to bypass traditional media channels and address his base effectively. His campaign also leveraged social media to fundraise, organize events, and counter criticisms from opponents.

Another key aspect of Trump's strategy was his emphasis on election integrity. He frequently discussed alleged irregularities and fraud in the 2020 election, framing these issues as a central part of his 2024 campaign. This rhetoric aimed to energize his base and cast himself as a champion for electoral reform. Trump's insistence on these claims contributed to his campaign's messaging and strategy.

Key Developments and Events

The 2024 campaign was marked by several significant developments and dramatic events. One of the most shocking incidents was an assassination attempt on Trump during a campaign rally.

On July 13, 2024, Trump was at a rally in Butler Township, Pennsylvania, when a gunshot grazed his ear. The assassination attempt shocked the nation and heightened security concerns for Trump and his campaign. The campaign chose not to disclose Trump's medical records, leading to speculation about his health and recovery. The incident highlighted the intense and often dangerous nature of contemporary political campaigns.

Despite the assassination attempt, Trump's campaign continued with high energy. The 2024 Republican National Convention, held shortly after the attack, nominated Trump as their presidential candidate. Senator JD Vance was selected as his running mate, solidifying the ticket for the upcoming election. The convention served as a platform for Trump to reaffirm his candidacy and appeal to Republican voters.

Throughout the campaign, Trump's rhetoric became increasingly polarizing. He made more frequent and aggressive statements about his opponents and continued to push the narrative of a "rigged" election. This rhetoric not only resonated with his supporters but also drew criticism from opponents and the media.

The campaign also faced legal and political challenges. In December 2023, the Colorado Supreme Court disqualified Trump from the Colorado Republican primary due to his involvement in the January 6, 2021, Capitol attack. However, in March 2024, the U.S.

The Supreme Court restored his name to the ballot, ruling that Colorado could not uphold the 14th Amendment of Section 3, which prohibits insurrectionists from running for federal office. This ruling was a significant development in Trump's campaign, ensuring his participation in the primary race.

Campaign Dynamics and Media Coverage

Trump's campaign was characterized by intense media coverage and frequent controversies. His approach to handling the media was similar to his previous campaigns, utilizing a combination of direct communication and confrontational rhetoric. Trump often criticized mainstream media outlets, labeling them as biased and corrupt.

The campaign debates and public appearances were marked by sharp exchanges and contentious discussions. Trump's opponents, including President Joe Biden and other Democratic candidates, frequently criticized his record and legal troubles.

The debates became arenas for heated exchanges on policy issues, personal conduct, and the future direction of the country.

In addition to debates, Trump's campaign held numerous rallies and public events, which were often used to galvanize support and generate media attention. These events were notable for their large crowds and enthusiastic supporters, reflecting Trump's continued influence among his base.

Chapter 6

Legacy and Public Impact

Donald Trump's time in office and his subsequent activities have had far-reaching effects on American culture, politics, and society. This chapter explores his lasting influence through his impact on popular culture and media portrayal, as well as his political and social legacy. We will examine how Trump's presidency has shaped U.S. politics, altered the dynamics within the Republican Party, and contributed to societal divisions.

Cultural Impact: Influence on Popular Culture and Media Portrayal

Media Representation

Donald Trump's presence in the media has been profound and multifaceted. His approach to communication, characterized by frequent, direct engagement with the public via social media, transformed the landscape of American political reporting. Trump used Twitter as a platform to bypass traditional media filters, making bold statements and setting the agenda for news coverage. This method of communication allowed him to speak directly to his supporters and critics alike, often escalating controversies and shaping public discourse.

Trump's media strategy included frequent, often combative interactions with news organizations. His administration's adversarial relationship with the press was a defining feature of his presidency. He frequently labeled unfavorable coverage as "fake news" and attacked media outlets he deemed hostile.

This contentious dynamic altered how news organizations operated, with many outlets focusing more on Trump's statements and controversies to attract viewers and readers. This shift not only changed media practices but also amplified the polarization of news coverage, contributing to a fragmented media landscape.

The portrayal of Trump in the media has been highly polarized. Conservative outlets have frequently depicted him as a populist hero who challenges the establishment and fights for the interests of ordinary Americans. They have celebrated his achievements, such as tax reforms and deregulation, and defended his controversial policies and statements.

On the other hand, liberal and mainstream media have often criticized Trump's actions, rhetoric, and policies, portraying him as a divisive figure who undermines democratic norms and principles. This polarized media portrayal has reinforced existing political divides and influenced how different segments of the population view his presidency.

Influence on Popular Culture

Trump's impact on popular culture is evident in various forms of entertainment, including television, film, and music. His larger-than-life persona and the controversies surrounding his presidency have inspired numerous cultural references and artistic works.

Television shows and films have often used Trump as a character or a subject of satire. Programs such as "Saturday Night Live" and "The Simpsons" featured Trump in exaggerated, comedic roles, reflecting both the public's fascination with his persona and critical perspectives on his presidency.

These portrayals often highlighted his flamboyant style, controversial statements, and the chaos of his administration, using humor and satire to engage with and critique his impact on American politics.

In music, Trump's influence has been significant. Many artists have incorporated themes related to his presidency into their work, either supporting or criticizing his policies and behavior. Songs and music videos addressing issues such as immigration, social justice, and political corruption have often reflected the political climate of Trump's presidency. His persona has become a symbol in popular culture, representing broader themes and serving as a touchstone for discussions about politics and society.

Iconic Symbols and Imagery

Trump's presidency has generated a range of iconic symbols and imagery. The "Make America Great Again" (MAGA) hat, for example, became a powerful emblem of his campaign and presidency. This red hat, emblazoned with the slogan, became a visual shorthand for Trump's populist and nationalist agenda. It symbolized his appeal to voters who felt left behind by economic and political changes and became a recognizable symbol of his political movement.

Conversely, symbols of resistance and protest have also become associated with opposition to Trump.

The pink "pussyhats" from the Women's March, for example, represented a powerful visual statement against Trump's policies and rhetoric. These symbols of protest reflected broader societal reactions to his presidency and became part of the cultural conversation surrounding his time in office.

Political and Social Legacy: Long-Term Effects on U.S. Politics, Republican Party Dynamics, and Societal Divisions.

Impact on U.S. Politics

Donald Trump's presidency has had a profound and lasting impact on American politics. His unconventional style and populist rhetoric have reshaped the political landscape, influencing both his party and the broader political environment.

Trump's emphasis on populism and his critique of the political establishment resonated with many voters who felt disillusioned with traditional politics. His presidency demonstrated the power of populist rhetoric in shaping electoral outcomes and influencing policy debates. Issues such as trade, immigration, and foreign policy were framed in ways that appealed to his base, challenging established political norms and priorities.

Trump's tenure also highlighted the changing role of media in politics. His use of social media to communicate directly with the public bypassed traditional news channels and altered how political figures engage with voters.

This shift has had lasting implications for political campaigning and media relations, with future candidates and administrations likely to follow his example of direct communication and media management.

Changes in Republican Party Dynamics

Trump's influence on the Republican Party has been significant and transformative. His presidency marked a shift towards more populist and nationalist positions within the party, leading to a realignment of its base and political strategies.

Trump's approach to issues such as immigration, trade, and foreign policy represented a departure from traditional Republican positions.

His policies on border security, trade protectionism, and skepticism of international agreements became central to the party's platform during and after his presidency. This shift reflected a broader realignment within the Republican Party, with Trump's brand of populism gaining prominence over traditional conservative values.

The Republican Party also experienced internal divisions as a result of Trump's influence. His presidency created a rift between traditional Republicans and those aligned with his populist agenda. This divide has had implications for party unity and electoral strategy, influencing how Republicans approach policy and candidate selection in subsequent elections.

Trump's impact on the Republican Party is also evident in how the party has dealt with his legacy. Some Republicans have embraced his policies and rhetoric, seeking to continue his political agenda. Others have sought to distance themselves from his controversies and focus on rebuilding the party's image. This dynamic has shaped the party's response to contemporary political challenges and its strategy for future elections.

Societal Divisions and Polarization.

Trump's presidency has been associated with increased societal divisions and political polarization. His rhetoric and policies often amplified existing social and political divides, contributing to heightened tensions within American society.

One area of increased polarization is immigration. Trump's stringent immigration policies and rhetoric on border security sparked significant debates and disagreements over immigration reform. His approach, which included building a border wall and implementing travel bans, invoked strong reactions from both supporters and critics, deepening the divide over immigration issues.

Another aspect of societal division during Trump's presidency was his handling of racial and social justice issues. His comments and policies related to race and policing often sparked protests and debates.

The Black Lives Matter movement, which gained prominence during his tenure, faced intense opposition and criticism from Trump and his supporters. This conflict over race and justice highlighted broader societal tensions and contributed to increased polarization on these issues.

Trump's influence on societal divisions extended to political discourse. His rhetoric often polarized public opinion, with his supporters rallying around his statements and policies while his critics condemned them. This polarization has had lasting effects on political conversations and public attitudes, shaping how individuals engage with political issues and participate in civic life.

Conclusion

As we draw the final curtain on the life and career of Donald J. Trump, it becomes clear that his impact on American society and politics is both profound and complex. From his early days as a brash real estate developer to his unprecedented presidency and beyond, Trump's journey reflects a unique confluence of ambition, controversy, and influence that has left an indelible mark on the nation.

Throughout this biography, we've explored the multifaceted dimensions of Trump's life: his rise from the shadow of his father's business to becoming a household name in real estate and entertainment; his dramatic and often polarizing entry into politics; and the far-reaching consequences of his time in office. We've examined how his policies, rhetoric, and personal style reshaped American political discourse and how his post-presidency years continue to stir debate and redefine his legacy.

Trump's story is not just about one man but also about the broader currents of American society that he both shaped and was shaped by. His presidency challenged established norms, disrupted traditional party lines, and polarized public opinion. His influence extends beyond the political arena into cultural and social realms, making his life a compelling study of modern American politics.

In reflecting on Trump's legacy, it's essential to recognize the enduring questions his career has raised about leadership, democracy, and public trust. Whether seen as a transformative figure or a controversial disruptor, Trump has undeniably altered the landscape of American politics and left a legacy that will be scrutinized and debated for years to come.

As you end your journey into this book, be reminded that understanding the complexities of such a figure requires more than just recounting events; it involves grappling with the broader implications of his actions and their impact on the world.

Donald J. Trump's life story is a testament to the power of individual influence and how personal ambition can intersect with national and global affairs.

In the end, Trump's journey is a mirror reflecting the hopes, fears, and divisions of contemporary America. It is a reminder that history is often written by those who dare to challenge the status quo and that the legacy of such figures will continue to provoke discussion and reflection long after their time in the spotlight has faded.

Printed in Great Britain
by Amazon

3e610733-1de3-4df6-85a5-6d92e6538831R01